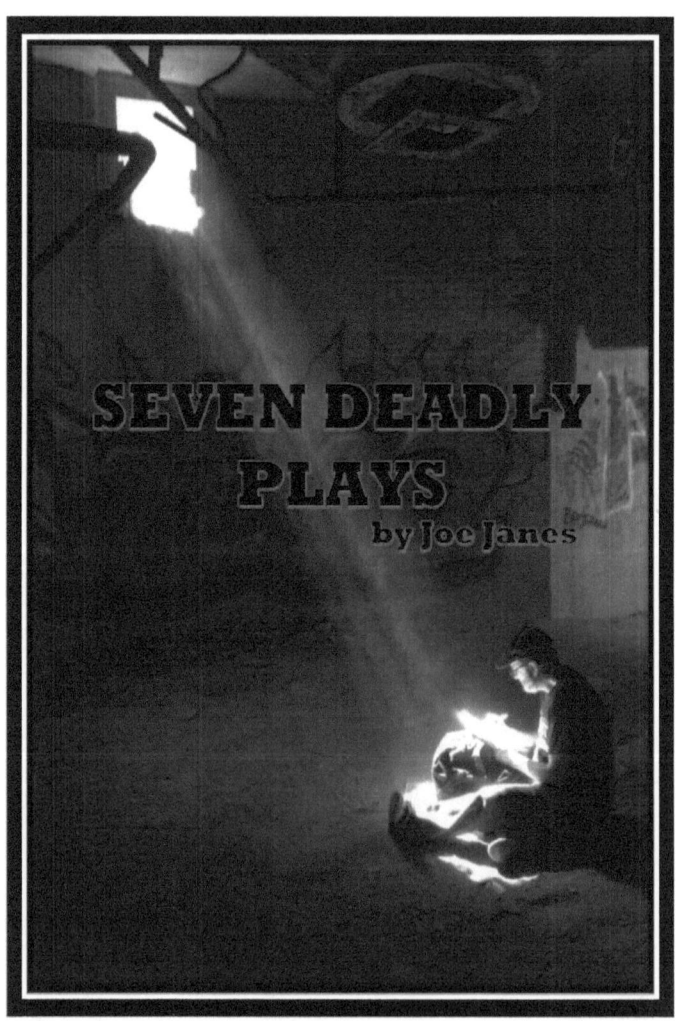

SEVEN DEADLY
PLAYS
by Joe Janes

ISBN: 978-1-304-43089-2

Bite And Smile Publications

Published and distributed through Lulu.com

Photo Composite by Don Hall

First Printing

All the plays were written by Joe Janes

One a day for a week.

The first play was written Thursday, August 16 2012

The last play was written Wednesday, August 21, 2012

They all debuted the evening of Thursday, August 22, 2012

Technical Director/Stage Manager: Dianna Driscoll Assisted by John Pagano

Produced by Don Hall and Joe Janes

Special thanks to Strawdog Theatre and Hank Boland

*denotes member of The Actors' Equity Association

BONUS CUTS

4

About Seven Deadly Plays

First off, it has nothing to do with the sins. The sins only helped give us a
fun title. The "deadly" refers to risky locations. The game I set up for myself
was to set seven different ten minute plays in seven different actual
Chicago area locales. For each place, I met with the director and cast and
we paid a visit. In this case, it was a speedboat on Lake Michigan during an
Air and Water Show rehearsal, an urban farm in a notoriously violent south
side neighborhood, an abandoned grain silo, a haunted cemetery, a
funhouse maze, up in a tree and in the back of a packed van driving around
Chicago traffic on lower Wacker. Once I got a sense of a place and took
some notes, I went off and wrote the script and sent it off to the director and
cast the very next morning. So, the first group had a full week to put their
piece together before opening night. The last group had the day of to prep
for the show that night. The deadlines added to the risk and made things
very exciting.

Of course, this project would not have been possible without an amazing
group of talented actors and directors up for the challenge and close friends
quick to recommend highly precarious places to set my ass.

As in all things done quickly and improvisationally, things changed as I
went. We were originally lined up to visit St. James Cathedral's bell tower
and the ball pit at the Chicago Children's Museum. They both fell through
the Monday morning we were to dive into the ball pit. Someone higher up
the food chain at the museum got wind we were going to be there and sent a
"no" back down to the people who work there. There's a special shout out to
them in the Funhouse piece. A big special thank you to Mike at the
Funhouse Maze who didn't hesitate to let us visit there. He was incredibly
supportive and just a super nice fun guy. The folks at St. James wanted us
to sign waivers in case someone got hurt. Not a problem until they asked us
if we had any waivers. Then they said it might take a few weeks for lawyers
to draft one, would we mind waiting? Um. Yep. We mind. We're on a tight
schedule. Ended up going to another high place, the tree in John Jughead
Pierson's front yard, which was a delightful experience. Climbing trees is
fun!

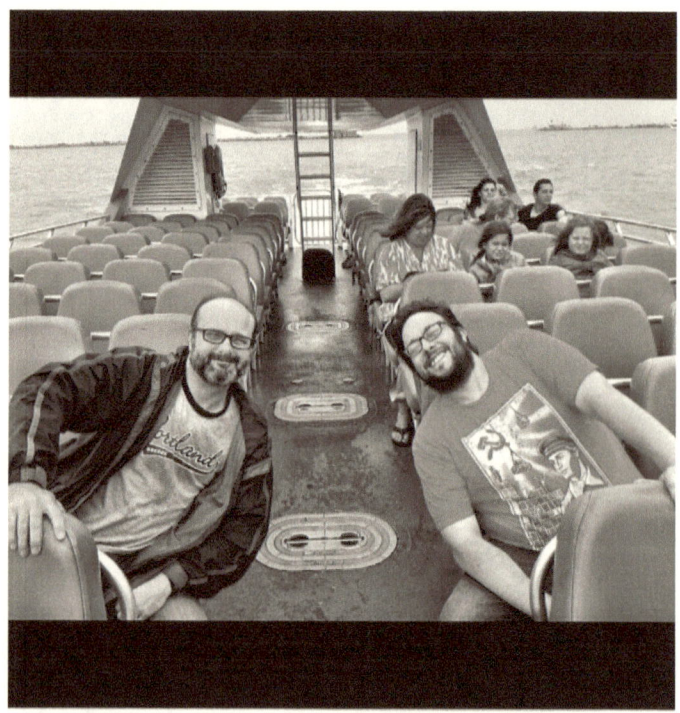

(Me with director Jason A. Fleece on the Seadog Speedboat off of Navy Pier. The genuinely funny wannabe stand-up tour guide took the pic. As you can see, the boat wasn't too crowded. It was also a rainy day which put a slight damper on their usual crowd. It was also the day before the Air and Water show so we were treated to low flying jets which added to the sense of danger.)

"Speedboat"
Written by Joe Janes

CAST:
Fenster, 20s
Grant, 20s
Captain Dianna, 20s

(In the dark, we hear *We Need A Hero* as we hear wind rushing and a high-speed motor boat's engines at full. If possible, the audience feels wind and the spray of water. We can also hear the laughter and squeals of Fenster as she enjoys the ride. We can also hear Grant "whoo-ing" in extreme delight. The engines cut and slow down. The music fades as lights come up. We see Fenster standing downstage in a yellow windbreaker and shorts. She speaks into a microphone. She engages with the audience as if they are the passengers on the speedboat tour. We also see Grant, in the audience, has been standing up video taping his face having too much of a good time. He looks a little wild eyed, soaked, and as if he has been riding on the boat all day. He carries a small opaque beat up Tupperware tub. He and Fenster exchange a few "whoo's" until he gets the hint from her to sit down.)

FENSTER: Whoo! Did you enjoy that? Wasn't that extreme? I'm Fenster and this is your Seadog Extreme speedboat tour! Whoo! That was just the first part of our tour. Looks like some of you got a little soaked. I warned you, didn't I? I did, I did. Hey, behind you, at the wheel, is Captain Dianna. She's the one who is getting you all wet. Everybody turn and wave to Captain Dianna! She's nicer than she looks. Say this with me! Yes! (She waits for the response.) Yes! (Response) Yes! (Response) Yes! Yes! Yes! (She waits for the response.) That was the first part of our Seadog speedboat tour of Lake Michigan. Arrrrrrrrrrrrrrrruff! (She waits for the audience to do it, too. If they do not, she repeats it until they do.) There you go! We're all seadogs, now! Right behind me and to the left you can see what was once the world's tallest building. The Willis Tower. It is still the tallest building-

GRANT: In the western hemisphere!

FENSTER: That's right. The western hemisphere. Has anyone visited the Willis Tower? Have you? Raise your hand, if you have. Great, great. The view is certainly extreme, but you know what I like?

GRANT: The bathrooms! You like the bathrooms!

FENSTER: Right. I do. Because-

GRANT: Because they're the highest bathrooms in the western hemisphere! Wheee!

FENSTER: Grant.

GRANT: Yes?

FENSTER: Grant. I'm... Have you been riding the boat all day?

GRANT: A little.

FENSTER: Ladies and gentlemen. We have a special guest. This is Grant. One of Seadog Extreme's biggest fans.

GRANT: I like them on Facebook!

FENSTER: He and his father ride the speedboat every weekend. Right, Grant?

GRANT: Just about.

FENSTER: Where's your dad?

GRANT: Oh, he's here.

FENSTER: He is? I don't see him. I hope he didn't go for a walk! (She laughs.) He didn't go for a walk, did he?

GRANT: No. Nope. He's here. Right here.

FENSTER: In that a Tupperware container?

GRANT: Yeah. It's not as bad as it looks. He's dead.

FENSTER: Oh, Grant. I'm so sorry. And he's in... there?

GRANT: It's okay. It's cool. Don't mean to bring everybody down. Not when we're having so much fun! Whoo! You should tell them about the, uh, museums, over there. That one. The aquarium. They have fish. In tanks. And in the restaurant. Which is weird. Don't look at me!

(He starts to cry. Fenster comes over to comfort him.)

FENSTER: Oh, Grant. Just let it out. Let it out. (He does. Oh, man, he does. Enormously.) Careful, you're splashing people.

GRANT: I just miss him so much. He wasn't just my father. He was my best friend. You know? You know what I mean? That point in your life when you realize your parents aren't just parents, but people. Human beings who had lives before you came along. Real lives, just like you have. And they start telling you about stuff they did and were into when they were your age, but not in a "you better learn from me" way but in a "man, we have a lot in common" way. Or a, "your old man did some cool things" way. Because he did. My dad did cool things. He met Elvis. Before Elvis was fat.

8

And he kissed Elizabeth Taylor. Before she was fat. And before he met my mom who has maintained her figure. We had just got to that point.

FENSTER: I just saw Charlie last week, Grant. It must have been sudden.

GRANT: Oh, God. One second he's making French toast with challah bread and almond slices and strawberries and the next, he's on the floor clutching his chest with one hand, holding on to a batter dipped spatula with the other. Trying to lick it. It was his heart. His big old stinking heart. I can't believe he's gone.

FENSTER: You two really loved coming out here.

GRANT: Yeah, we did. (To the other "tourists") This place creates memories. Memories for life. Extreme memories. Memories until you no longer have a life. Cherish them. Our favorite times to come out here were just before or after a thunderstorm and the clouds look so ominous. Or during the air and water show with all the jets coming in so low.

FENSTER: Charlie was a lovely man.

GRANT: He and my mom met at Navy Pier. She used to work at the Dippin' Dots stand.

FENSTER: The ice-cream of the future.

GRANT: They met back when now was the future. He worked nearby. He used to engrave people's names and faces onto the sides of churros. When he proposed to her, he did it by slipping a diamond ring on a cinnamon churro and carving "Will you marry me?" on it.

FENSTER: That's so romantic.

GRANT: She broke a tooth. But she still said "yes." Or, rather, "yeth."

FENSTER: Maybe you should be home with your mother, Grant. She probably needs you.

GRANT: She does need me. She sent me here. On a mission. These are my father's ashes. It was his wish to have them dumped into the lake from this very boat.

FENSTER: Oh.

GRANT: You're not going to let me do it, are you? The last three tour guides wouldn't let me, either.

FENSTER: It's littering. Technically.

GRANT: How can someone call my father's ashes litter?

FENSTER: The Coast Guard can. And if they see it, they'll fine us thousands of dollars and I'd lose my job.

GRANT: "If" they see it? Sounds like you want this as much as I do, Fenster.

FENSTER: Well-

GRANT: You were his favorite. He always said it was always a better day when you led our boat tour.

FENSTER: Well, you guys won't tell will you? Will you? Captain Dianna? (Captain Dianna shrugs.) Okay, but let's do this real quick.

GRANT: Thank you. Thank you. This means the world to me. (Grant gets up and moves to the bow of the boat with Fenster. He takes the lid off the Tupperware and gets ready to pour it over the side.

FENSTER: Wait. (She looks around.) Okay. I think we're good.

GRANT: Uh. I should say something.

FENSTER: Okay. Hurry.

GRANT: No. You should. He loved this boat. He loved you.

FENSTER: He loved me?

GRANT: He always said you were like the daughter he never had and only saw briefly on weekends.

FENSTER: Oh. Wow. I'm a little choked up. Um. Here, in this tiny plastic box, are the ashes of Charlie. Keeping fresh his heart and soul. His love for adventure. His love for his family. His love for fried foods. We will miss him, won't we? Yes! (Waits for response) Yes! (Waits for response) Yes! Yes! Yes!

   (Grant pours the ashes over the side, but only the slightest amount comes out.)

FENSTER: Your father is much smaller in death.

GRANT: Oh, no. I think I lost most of him. Oh, no. He must have leaked out.

FENSTER: Is it under your seat?

GRANT: No.

FENSTER: Where were you earlier?

GRANT: I don't know. I moved around a lot. I thought I'd have to sneak pouring the ashes over.

FENSTER: Ladies and gentlemen, please look under your seat for Charlie. Please, just take a look. Does anyone see Charlie?

GRANT: Please help me find my father!

(They do this until someone finds Charlie's remains, a moist pile of clay or dough, planted under their seat.)

FENSTER: Oh, no. The ashes must have gotten wet from all the spray.

GRANT: Dad!

(Grant cradles the turd-like remains like something that needs gentle care.)

FENSTER: Hurry up, Charlie, while the Coast Guard is still on the other side of that party boat over there.

(Grant holds the lump over the side.)

GRANT: Dad. I love you. You were the best dad a son could ever have. I'll do my best to take care of mom. I'll do my best to carry on in your footsteps by working at Navy Pier. As soon as we dock, I'll go back over to Bubba Gump Shrimp and see if they have looked at my application yet. You always loved the Seadog Extreme Tour. You said it made you feel like you were flying. Fly away, Dad. Fly away.

(Grant lobs the lump as if he were setting a bird free. It plops to the floor, of course. What with gravity and all. Do I really need to explain that?)

FENSTER: Look. He's floating.

GRANT: Right. He's floating.

(Grant puts his arm around Fenster as they look at the lump. He realizes he has done this. They look at each other for a moment.)

GRANT: I think my dad would have wanted me to jam my tongue down your throat, right now.

FENSTER: Of course, he would. I was like a daughter to him.

(They kiss passionately. And sloppily. They break apart.)

FENSTER and GRANT: ARRRRRRrrrrrrrrrrrrrrrrrrrrRUFF!

FENSTER: Get back in that seat, mister.

GRANT: Aye-aye, tour guide Fenster.

(He goes back to his seat.)

FENSTER: We're about to take off on the next part of our extreme tour! Hit it, Captain Dianna!

(The engines roar to life. A beefed up version of *Gonna Fly Now* starts playing. Fenster gets everyone to raise their hands up in the air as the lights fade. More water spritzing. The end.)

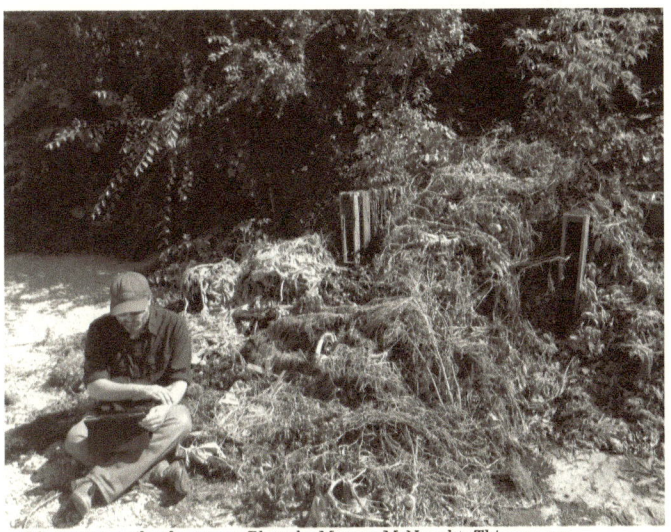

(Me next to a pile of compost. Photo by Morgan McNaught. This was my
first visit to the Chicago neighborhood known as Englewood. It is notorious
for its gang violence. I also got lost getting there via public transportation
adding to my unease. The thing is, the place was like being at the for real
happiest place on earth. It was very serene and everyone we spoke to loved
the place. It's called Growing Home. Their urban and rural farms have an
educational and vocational aspect where they train ex-convicts and
formerly homeless people in developing job skills. You should give them lots
of money and buy organic produce from them. I have since been to the
Englewood farm many times, often riding my bike there. It's not that scary
any more. During the day.)

"Urban Farm, Englewood"
written by Joe Janes

CAST:
Jenni, 40s
Ruth, 30s
Alee, 20s

(This should be done in the style of an overly melodramatic production of
Chekhov's *The Three Sisters* sans dialects. The characters have a heavy
layer of sadness that they are unable to hide. Lights up on Jenni picking
radishes from the ground and placing them into a plastic crate. She is doing
this methodically and thoughtfully. Almost a form of meditation. She does
this in silence for a bit. Digging fingers around a radish and gently pulling
the vegetable from the dirt. Ruth enters with a bucket of water. She sits
near the plastic crate. She takes radishes and puts them into the bucket to
soak. She pulls them out, making sure the water has relieved the radish
and its greens of dirt and insects. She places each radish gently into
another crate to dry. Alee enters. She takes processed radishes and ties
them together with a long twisty in groups of three. By the way, this can all
be done via object work without any props. But it must be done with
meticulous detail. Each radish is its own unique entity.)

RUTH: It's a beautiful day.

JENNI: Every day is a beautiful day in its own way.

(Alee processes another three radishes in silence.)

RUTH: Today is more beautiful than yesterday.

JENNI: I liked yesterday's clouds.

ALEE: And the rain. The rain is always beautiful.

(Alee processes more radishes in silence.)

RUTH: The rain is always beautiful.

JENNI: Always. Beautiful.

(They stay very still as they hear in the far distance tires screech and a car
crash, a car alarm and some gun shots. The alarm shuts off abruptly. They
go back to harvesting and processing radishes.)

RUTH: These radishes are the best radishes we have ever pulled from the
dirt.

ALEE: So round and plump.

14

JENNI: And firm.

RUTH: It's the color. The most vibrant red I have ever seen. I want to kiss them.

JENNI: You're crazy.

ALEE: And weird. Mostly crazy.

RUTH: I don't care. Look up crazy in the dictionary. It's a good thing.

JENNI: Crazy means crazy.

ALEE: Pretty clear.

RUTH: You have to go deeper. To the third or fourth definition. After insanity, it means "intensely enthusiastic, passionately excited." Those are good things to be.

JENNI: I don't like dictionaries.

ALEE: They're so full of themselves.

          (Jenni is finished picking radishes. she stands and stretches.)

RUTH: What shall we pick tomorrow?

ALEE: The tomatoes should be ready.

JENNI: I don't want to think about tomorrow.

RUTH: The tomatoes should be ready.

JENNI: I don't want to think about tomorrow. Can't count on anything these days. Can't count on anything at all. All you can count on is right now.

(In the distance, they hear a police siren go by. Then a firetruck. Then an ambulance. Then an ice-cream truck. They are still while this happens.)

JENNI: You are none of those things.

RUTH: What?

JENNI: Intensely enthusiastic or passionately excited.

RUTH: Yes, I am. I really am. I may not show it. But I am. In here. All the time. All the time. (She is nearly in tears.)

ALEE: What are you intensely enthusiastic about?

RUTH: Life. (Jenni laughs. Alee joins in.) This place, then. I love what I do here. I'm happy.

JENNI: Oh.

ALEE: I'm happy, too.

JENNI: I forget that I'm happy.

ALEE: Right?

JENNI: But since you have reminded me. Yes. I'm happy. I love this farm.

RUTH: Me, too!

ALEE: Me, too!

RUTH: I want to be buried here. Right here. Between the radishes and the garlic.

ALEE: When you die?

RUTH: Then, too.

JENNI: This farm is my lover.

ALEE: Now, who's crazy?

JENNI: Not me.

ALEE: I didn't mean anything...

JENNI: I dig my fingers into it's dirty back.

RUTH: I did want to kiss the radishes. And the zucchini do make me blush so.

ALEE: I love the smells. (She inhales deeply.) That peppery, earthy smell. Especially after the rain.

RUTH: And I love... I love the two of you.

ALEE: I love the two of you.

JENNI: I only love one of you and, really, not all that much. But enough. And I effectively tolerate the other, which is a form of love, I suppose. And it doesn't make me any less happy.

RUTH: Or me.

ALEE: Or...me.

(In the far distance they hear an airplane, a bomb drop and a nuclear explosion. Very faint. Followed by warning sirens. As this happens, they move to one another and hold one another. The warning sirens fade.)

JENNI: The carrots should be big, again, this year.

ALEE: Really big.

RUTH: And sentient.

(Lights fade to black.)

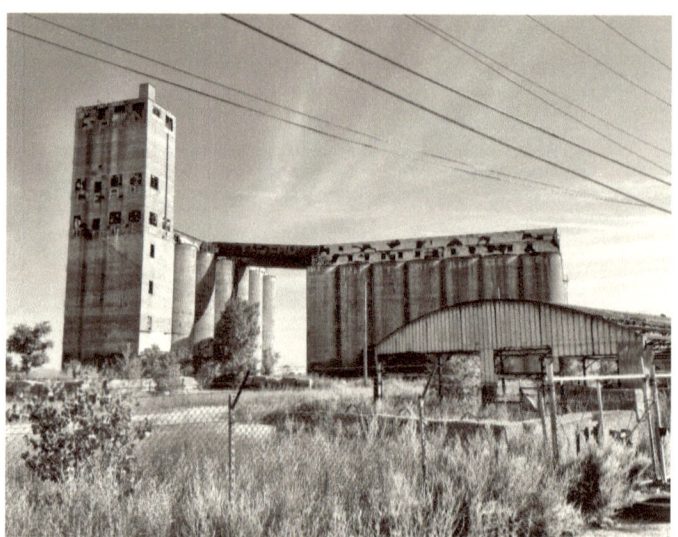

(The abandoned Damen Silos. 14 stories tall. If you have driven on I-55
near the Loop, you have seen it. We climbed up the inside of the silos on the
right, crossed over in the covered passageway and then climbed a fire
escape up to the top on the left. The most physically dangerous place I
visited. A homeless guy named Gone had set up an apartment and a
garden. Since then, the police have really cracked down on transients and
casual trespassers. Some of the graffiti is quite amazing. On on-line search
will take you to many breathtaking images. My friend Faraz recommended
it and gave us a tour. There are many nooks and crannies and hidden
treasures. The things mentioned in the play were actually found there.)

"The Damen Silos"
Written by Joe Janes

CAST:
Stephanie
Reeny
Andy

(The stage is dark. Stephanie enters in the dark. We see light spill in from the door she opens and then closes. We hear her set her backpack down and open it. She takes out some books and notebooks and a candlestick and holder. She lights the candle. That's right. She lights it. She is upset. On the verge of tears. She starts to write in one of her journals. From offstage we hear...)

REENY (off): Andy! This place is so cool!

ANDY (off): I told you!

REENY (off): How come you know so many cool places?

ANDY (off): Because I'm so cool.

(Reeny opens the door and sticks her head in.)

REENY: What's in here?

ANDY: I don't know. I've never been in this part of the building. (He turns on his cell phone flashlight.) There's no daylight in here.

(Reeny turns hers on and looks inside the room.)

REENY: Doesn't look like there's any graffiti on the walls.

ANDY: Too dark. Why put art where no one will see it?

(They both walk into the room.)

REENY: This whole building is so awesome. It's like exploring a ruins.
Ruin? A ruined?

ANDY: A ruined. I like that, Reeny. This abandoned grain silo is equal parts creepy and cool. And right next to a canal. You'd think someone would have bought this place and turned it into something or other.

REENY: Sounds like a sound business plan.

ANDY: At least make it a haunted house. It's begging to be haunted.

19

REENY: You know we're doing everything anyone in a horror film would do to get killed? You know that, don't you?

        (Andy moves in to hold and kiss Reeny.)

ANDY: Don't worry, baby, I'll protect you.

REENY: Now we're doomed for certain.

ANDY: As long as we don't have sex here, we're fine. (He moves in on her, again.) Cuz that's totally not going to happen, right-

REENY: Hey, what's that?

(They both turn their flashlights to Stephanie who continues to write while crying. They don't see or hear her.)

ANDY: Looks like a homeless guy left some stuff.

REENY: What if they're still here? We should go.

        (Andy does a sweep around the room with his flashlight.)

ANDY: I think we're okay. The candle's all burnt out. Look, it's all books.

REENY: Textbooks. Mostly. (She opens the backpack and rifles through it.) Hey, a comic book.

ANDY: Graphic novel.

REENY: That's what I said. Comic book. *Fallen Angel*?

ANDY: Never heard of it. Oh, my God. Look at this. It's a journal. (He opens it and Reeny reads over his shoulder.)

REENY: We shouldn't-

STEPHANIE: December 30, 2010. 1:30am.

ANDY: 1:30am.

STEPHANIE: I'm afraid too much. Reaching out to people is too scary and difficult. It's too cold.

REENY: Oh, my God. Do you think someone died here?

ANDY: What? No. I mean, it doesn't look like it. If there was a dead body found here, they would have taken all her stuff, right?

REENY: That's what they would have done on *Law and Order.*

ANDY: Exactly.

(They go back to reading.)

STEPHANIE: I guess I just got so used to Jasmine being around. All the phone calls, the e-mails back and forth, all the late night therapy sessions. I just got used to a particular way of us being together. Especially after leaving my mother and putting my family behind me. I felt so fragile and Jasmine helped. She helped me. She helped me.

ANDY: Do you think she's a lesbian?

REENY: Why does your mind automatically go there?

ANDY: Well, Sherlock, who is Jasmine to this woman?

REENY: How do you know she's a woman?

ANDY: She sounds like a woman.

REENY: Really.

ANDY: And Hello Kitty on the cover of the journal increases the odds.

REENY: I so don't want you to be right.

(We hear a cell phone ring. It's Stephanie's. She picks up.)

STEPHANIE: Mom?... Hi.. No, everything's fine... I'm fine... Work's good... Really... Why would I lie about whether or not work is good?... I wish I could have come home over the break, too... A girl's gotta work... I've got to go... Because it's 1:30 in the morning, Mom. On a Thursday... Yes. It is. Look at the clock in the kitchen... Look at the clock in the kitchen... I don't know, I don't know where the time goes... Yeah.... Yeah.... Yeah... Me, too... me, too... No. No, I don't want to talk to... Hi, Chuck... Yep. My mom's something... Glad you two are continuing the holiday party... I really cannot understand what you are saying... It's Stephanie. Not Steffie. (She hangs up. She looks like she's about to cry, again. The phone rings. She looks at it and turns it off. She goes back to writing.)

ANDY: I think I know who Jasmine is.

STEPHANIE: I got so used to Jasmine that I never considered her feelings. How this might actually be affecting her. I thought I was her favorite. I liked her and therefore I thought she liked me. She made me feel special. Cared for. She made me feel loved. In a world where I have felt so little of that, I wanted more. It can be addictive. I had no idea I was "wearing her out."

ANDY: Teacher. She's a student. Got some special attention from a teacher. Teacher might even have been fishing for it. Blammo. They're doing it.

REENY: Again, too much porn. It could be so many other things.

ANDY: Jasmine delivers pizza?

REENY: She could be a therapist. A spiritual leader of some sorts. A neighbor, even.

ANDY: My porn's better than your porn.

STEPHANIE: Jasmine said I can't see her anymore. I've been trying to scrounge up enough money, but I've gotten behind in payments.

ANDY: Jasmine's a hooker.

REENY: No, she's not.

ANDY: Sounds like it. She's paying to see her. And, we missed the most important clue, her name is Jasmine.

REENY: I'm sticking with therapist.

ANDY: You say tomato, I say hooker.

REENY: This poor woman. Think about it. She's alone. Lonely. Trying to do things to make her life better. Yet she holes up here. Here. The middle of nowhere in the middle of the night in winter in a room with no light and pours her heart out into this book. Poor thing. A book we shouldn't even be reading. What the hell are we doing?

ANDY: I don't know, I mean, you're right. This is fucked up. But it's also from 2010. If she wanted to keep her secrets under wrap, why put them out in the open in the basement of an abandoned grain silo?

REENY: I'm not sure how to respond to that.

ANDY: I wonder what happened to her. Why did she leave her stuff behind?

STEPHANIE: I'm cold. Very cold. And tired. Exhausted. I thought someone loved me. I was wrong. Again. I want to stop trying. I'd kill myself, but I don't want to leave a mess. I can't stand the thought of someone finding my dead body. I hear you shit your pants when you die. No one should see that. No one should have to clean that up. (Reeny and Andy look at one another. Stephanie turns her phone back on. She hits speed dial for

22

someone and waits for them to answer.) Jasmine?... Hi... It's Stephanie... I
know. It's late. I'm so sorry... I know you're not technically my therapist any
more. I didn't know who else to call... Well, I'm thinking about killing
myself... A little... Um, sure. It can wait until morning. What am I going to
do? Go out and kill myself at this hour? Not worth getting out of bed for
that, right? ... Yeah, I still have that card you gave me for the free
services... No. I did. I did go. Once. He just didn't get me... And he smelled
funny.... He smelled like my stepdad... Like furniture polish... I went back
to using tarot cards- I get it... I get it... I SAID I GET IT! ... Jasmine, I'm so
sorry. I'm so sorry. Okay, good-bye. (She looks at the phone and puts it in
her pocket.)

REENY: Do you think she went through with it?

ANDY: I don't know. The rest of the book is blank.

REENY: Maybe there's another journal.

(Andy and Reeny get down on the ground and look through the books. As
they do, Stephanie blows out the candle, gets up and heads to the door.)

ANDY: These are all old ones.

REENY: Wait. This one goes back to 2006. Holy shit. "The Magickal
Journal of Stephanie Maureen Adkins. In Progress Eternal." Weird. It's full
of spells for summoning somebody named Balder.

ANDY: He's the Norse god of reconciliation.

REENY: How do you know that?

ANDY: I read it in a comic book.

REENY: I guess we'll never know what happened.

ANDY: Should we just leave her stuff?

REENY: I don't think we should take it.

ANDY: Yeah. You're right.

(They walk toward the door.)

REENY: Hey. Can I tell you something?

ANDY: Sure.

REENY: If you ever feel lonely or don't feel loved, I want you to remember
something. I love you.

ANDY: I love you, too.

REENY: Good. Let's keep it that way. Even after we break up.

(Reeny exits.)

ANDY: Wait. What?

(Andy follows. Closes door. The end.)

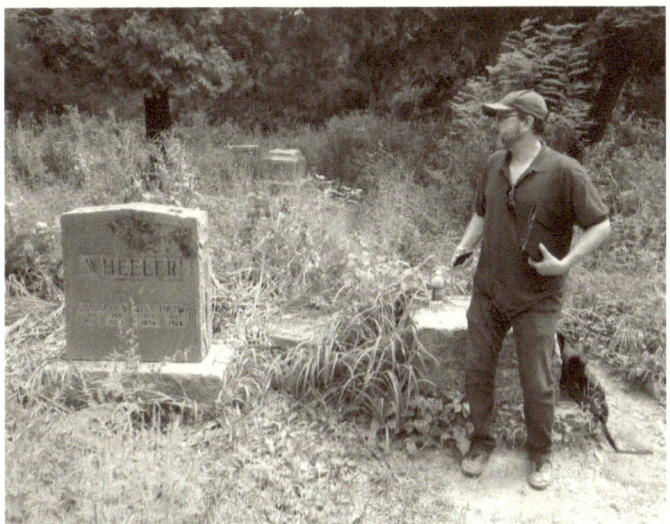

(In Bachelors Grove Cemetery, Bremen Township, Cook County, Illinois. The most haunted place on earth. Except on pleasant Sunday afternoons. Frank drove Faraz and me there. Faraz took this photo. We weren't quite sure where it was and ended up walking through a huge chunk of thick woods to get there and back to the car. You can almost make out the little green burrs on my shirt near my crotch. It's a creepy place, for sure. It's also next to a dead pond covered in scum. I think to get the full spooky effects of the place one has to be there at night. You can also find some interesting images on-line.)

"Bachelors Grove Cemetery"
Written by Joe Janes

CAST:
Ashley, 20s
Julie, 20s
Megan, 20s
Natalie, 20s

(Lights up on an abandoned cemetery during the day. There is overgrowth
and a smattering of headstones. Some knocked over. It is hilly. There is no
uniformity that we would expect from a cemetery. All four women are
spread throughout looking around. Natalie takes a tall PBR out of her
backpack and cracks it open. The rest all turn quickly to her at the noise.
She shrugs and they go back to looking. They read some headstones. For
some of these, they have to look sideways because they have been knocked
over. Yes, this all can be done through object work. Although an actual
backpack and real beer is probably a good idea.)

ASHLEY: Some of these headstones are ancient. This one goes back to
1914.

JULIE: Most of them are ancient.

MEGAN: Not this one, Jules. This dude was buried with his family in 1989.

JULIE: That's weird. That's not that long ago. How could this place fall to
such disarray since 1989?

NATALIE: That's fucked up.

JULIE: You'd think people would have learned after *Poltergeist*. Don't
disarray cemeteries. Array them. With love.

MEGAN: Except it wasn't because they moved the headstones and not the
bodies. In *Poltergeist*. It's because they built on top of an Indian burial
ground. It's in *Poltergeist 2*.

JULIE: I disavow the existence of *Poltergeist 2*. Pure bullshit that tarnishes
the reputation of the original.

MEGAN: You'd love *Poltergeist 3*, then. Takes place in the Hancock
building. I shit you not.

ASHLEY: We really shouldn't be talking about ghosts in a cemetery. This
place is supposed to be, you know...

JULIE: Haunted?

ASHLEY: Don't say it.

MEGAN: There aren't any ghosts, here. Just dirt and rocks and things that have been long dead. Here it is, Natalie. Guys. It's here!

NATALIE: Yep. That's it.

JULIE: Amazetta Curtis Warren. 1853-1878.

ASHLEY: Shit. She was only 25.

MEGAN: So, she's still buried here.

NATALIE: I guess.

MEGAN: It's just hard to tell. This is the most un-cemetery cemetery. It's hard to tell how things are supposed to be laid out.

NATALIE: Vandals messed up or jacked a lot of the headstones. And as the place was decaying, families pulled their peeps out and put them into nicer neighborhoods, but left the original headstones.

ASHLEY: This cemetery, like, died. How do you bury a cemetery?

NATALIE: Let it rot, apparently.

JULIE: How do you know Amazetta is still here?

NATALIE: I don't, really, except that she's not with the rest of the fam in the hoity-toity Whispering Hills. They moved everyone except her. (She points to a headstone near Amazetta's.) Even her husband, Ichabod Earl made the trip.

MEGAN: Ick, Ichabod.

ASHLEY: That sucks.

NATALIE: I suppose. For all we know, she's thrilled. Maybe her family was a bunch of dicks.

ASHLEY: That's your family.

NATALIE: Then they are a bunch of dicks. What do you know? Everybody take a beer. (She passes them out, Ashley declines.) Take it.

JULIE: Ashley doesn't drink.

ASHLEY: I drink.

JULIE: Appletinis don't count.

ASHLEY: I drink beer. I just don't like that kind. I'm really picky about beer. Not me, personally. My body is.

MEGAN: Just take one, Ash. It's symbolic.

NATALIE: Just take one sip and I'll take care of the rest. Or make you chug it like I did in Dante Bell's basement junior year of high school.

ASHLEY: That's why I don't drink that swill, Natalie.

MEGAN: You shouldn't have eaten chopped suey that night.

JULIE: Megan. It's just chop suey. Not chopped suey.

MEGAN: But they chop it, don't they? I thought that's how it got its name. The vegetables aren't whole. You don't get a whole unchopped cow when you order the beef.

NATALIE: You're not going to win this one.

ASHLEY (TAKING THE BEER): Fine. Let's do this. This place gives me the creeps.

MEGAN: They're coming to get you, Julie.

JULIE: Don't even.

NATALIE: Shut it. Raise your beers. To Amazetta-

ASHLEY: To Amazetta!

NATALIE: I'm not done yet.

ASHLEY: Sorry.

NATALIE: To Amazetta. I found you. My family may have forgotten about you through the years. Or tried to keep you buried in the past. But I'm here to tell you, you are remembered, Amazetta. We are here to honor your spirit. To declare that you lived and a century plus later, you live on in us. I know about you. To most people, you're just a name hidden deep in the roots of the family tree with an asterisk. Cause and year of death unknown. We now know when.

JULIE: I wonder how she died.

28

MEGAN: We don't know.

ASHLEY: It was the 1800s. It could have been the plague.

NATALIE: Nobody knows where or how you died. We're pretty sure it wasn't the plague. I'd like to think you went out with a bang. Robbed a bank, maybe. Set City Hall on fire.

JULIE: Punched Hitler in the face.

NATALIE: Hitler wasn't born yet.

JULIE: Even better. Punch that murdering zygote.

NATALIE: Good one.

MEGAN: Stole a horse and carriage and went on a drunken joy ride over a cliff. (They all look at her.) While it was on fire. Filled with explosives.

NATALIE: Nice.

ASHLEY: Killed while trying to escape jail.

NATALIE: Why was she in jail?

ASHLEY: Oh, you know. Because she did something women weren't supposed to do at the time. Kissed a strange man on the lips in the street. Wore a skirt above her ankle. Voted.

NATALIE: Amazetta. You were a bad ass. To Amazetta. (They raise their cans and drink. Ashley takes small, small sips. There's a long pause.)

JULIE: I was half expecting her ghost to appear. Would have been perfect timing.

MEGAN: Why would a ghost haunt a cemetery? Really? Great for movies, but really? Dumbest place ever to haunt. It's not where they died. It's not their home. They don't have memories here. You only get to torment strangers if you're in this place. You don't even get to spy on people taking showers or having sex. Sure. It's where their bones are, but why would you want to hang around a bunch of dried up bones? If there are ghosts here, they haunt the place because they're bored. Right, ghosts? Right?

(There's another pause.)

JULIE: Thought for sure that would work.

NATALIE: Maybe ghosts don't work that way. Maybe they're smarter than that.

29

ASHLEY: I never considered ghosts having an IQ.

NATALIE: Why not? Look, a ghost that pops up and scares you? Well, that's rude and not very imaginative. Maybe Amazetta's a ghost. She somehow figured out a way for me to notice she existed and influenced me to find her. She got rejected by her family. My family hates me. They do. They fucking do. Maybe she wanted someone she could connect with. Someone she can reach out to. Intelligently. No balls of light, no mist, no rattling chains or shouting "Boo!" She's not a drama queen. She's smart. I'm smart. She knew I'd figure shit out without having to go all *Poltergeist*. Way to go, Amazetta. You rock.

MEGAN: That deserves another toast. (They all drink.)

(Another pause.)

(Julie is about to speak when they hear a very low volume whispery "thank you." The ladies all stand there frozen. Natalie shrugs and takes a drink.)

NATALIE

Bad ass.

(The lights fade as everyone except Natalie slowly starts to back away. The End.)

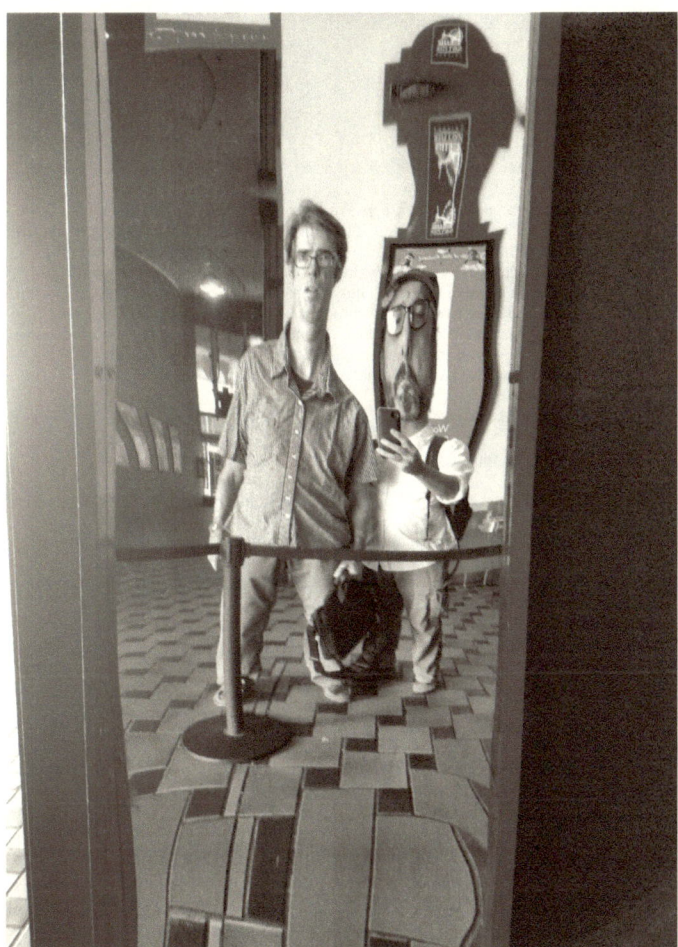

(Will Clinger and I at the Funhouse Maze at Navy Pier. Sadly, his body really does look like that. We were set to meet at the Children's Museum and that literally got canceled at the last minute. The folks at the Funhouse Maze welcomed us. We had a blast.)

31

"Funhouse Maze"
Written by Joe Janes

CAST:
Mr. Pickles, 50s
Zach, 30s
Jack, 40s
Tony, 20s

(Lights up on an empty stage. We hear a buzz sound and then we see Jack pushing Tony onto the edge of the stage, holding him by the back of his suit jacket collar. They're a little dizzy having just emerged from a spinning tunnel. They press sideways through inflated walls. Then they walk through a maze of mirrors. That's right. A maze of mirrors. This is, of course, all done through environment work. They both wear business suits. Tony is hugging a real briefcase. They are meticulous about each move they make. They even make a fasle turn and correct themselves. They finally reach a clearing and Jack pushes Anthony to the floor.)

JACK: Make yourself comfy.

TONY: I'm telling you, Jack. I wasn't going anywhere.

JACK: I know you aren't. I do not know for a fact that you weren't.

TONY: We have an appointment. For tomorrow. I wouldn't miss that.

JACK: Tony. You can understand why I'm a little suspicious. You haven't exactly kept your word with Mervin.

TONY: That was just a misunderstanding.

JACK: It was just a misappropriating. Of funds.

TONY: Funds that I was already misappropriating for Mervin-

JACK: Mister Pickles. You have forfeited the right to call him by his first name.

TONY: Fine, fine. Mr. Pickles. I was keeping the funds skimmed from the merry-go-rides and the Ferris wheel and the funhouse longer than usual to beef up the interest. That's all.

JACK: You can explain it to Mervin when he gets here. (Jack takes out phone and dials.)

TONY: Really? Come on, Jack. There's no need to bring Mr. Pickles into this. I'll meet you tomorrow with the money and everything will be good. It'll be good, again. You'll see.

32

JACK: No more tomorrows. Today. (Into phone) I'm in the funhouse with Tony. After the spinning tunnel, go through the squishy walls and through the maze. We're in the clearing on the other side. (He hangs up and gives Tony a "now you're gonna get it" look. We hear a buzz sound and see Mr. Pickles dramatically enter where Tony and Jack entered and he's also a little dizzy. But he musters up his bad guy attitude before he squeezes through the inflated walls. He goes through the maze, exactly how they went through it, even making the false turn. He gets to the center.)

TONY: Mr. Pickles!

(Mr. Pickles holds up his finger warning Tony to keep quiet. He doesn't say anything. He eyes Tony up and down. He takes Tony's briefcase by the handle.)

TONY: No. There's nothing in it. I swear.

(Mr. Pickles pulls harder. Tony releases it. He sets it on the floor. Both Mr. Pickles and Jack kneel down and open it. As it opens, light pours out of it like the briefcase in *Pulp Fiction*.)

TONY: If you don't mind. The batteries are about dead. (Tony reaches in and turns off the light.) I sometimes work in the dark.

    (Mr. Pickles reaches in and pulls out some papers. He stands and looks them over.)

MR. PICKLES: Hold him.

      (Jack makes Tony stand up. He gets behind him and secures him.)

TONY: This isn't necessary.

MR. PICKLES: Hold out his hand. (Jack forces Tony's right hand out.) Looks like you've been transferring a lot of money to an account in Costa Rica.

TONY: No. No! It's a tax haven. For you! All for you! Honest.

        (Mr. Pickles throws the papers down and approaches Tony.)

MR. PICKLES: The less you struggle, the less painful this will be.

(Tony tenses up and Mr. Pickles inspects his hand and forearm thoughtfully. Mr. Pickles reaches into his coat pocket and pulls out a nail file.)

TONY: You're going to give me a manicure?

MR. PICKLES: I am. Problem is. I'm not very good at it. Now, what have we here?

(Tony tries to pull his hand back. Mr. Pickles pulls it forward with a stern look. Tony gives in. Mr. Pickles starts giving Tony a manicure.)

TONY: That's really not so bad.

MR. PICKLES: No. Really. I try. But I'm just not that great at it. Look at how uneven your index finger is now. See? Now, Jack. Jack is good.

JACK: Thank you, Mervin.

TONY: You guys give each other manicures?

MR. PICKLES: All the time. Is that a problem?

TONY: No, no.

JACK: Pedicures, too.

MR. PICKLES: My feet used to be a mess. Now, it's like walking on butter. You should really take better care of your nails, Tony. You're a biter. Worst thing ever for your nails. Do you bite them because you're nervous?

TONY: Sometimes. Mostly, it's just a bad habit I've had since I was a kid.

MR. PICKLES: Bad habits are hard to break.

TONY: No kidding, ow, that hurts.

MR. PICKLES: It's going to hurt even more when you realize I'm only going to only manicure one hand. The left one will remain gangly. It's going to cause mental anguish.

(They hear that buzz sound.)

JACK: Someone's coming.

(We see Zach enter in a polo shirt and khakis. He goes through the maze exactly as the others did but with more confidence and skips the false turn.)

ZACH: Hey, guys.

MR. PICKLES: What is it, Zach? We're busy.

ZACH: Hey, don't mean to bother you. The boss has been getting on me about locking up the funhouse on time. And he stressed that I'm not allowed to have friends in here after hours. So, you know.

TONY: Son. I'm your boss.

ZACH: I know that, Dad. I just didn't want, you know, that nepotism thing to come up, again.

MR. PICKLES: We all know. But don't worry; we'll be out of here just as soon as your old man here tells us when we'll get our money.

TONY: I told Jack tomorrow.

MR. PICKLES: Oh, well, then. Aren't we the jerks? Let's just meet tomorrow. I'm not a fool, Tony. What's this? (Mr. Pickles pulls two plane tickets out of Tony's jacket pocket.)

TONY: It's nothing. It's nothing.

MR. PICKLES: Two one-way plane tickets to Costa Rica for tomorrow morning.

JACK: You don't do e-tickets?

MR. PICKLES: How are we to meet in the afternoon, if you're already gone?

TONY: They're not for me!

JACK: Do you really expect us to believe that?

ZACH: He's right. They're not for him. It's for me and my lover.

JACK: Are you gay?

ZACH: No. Lover can be a woman, too. Right?

TONY: Zach...

ZACH: We need to tell them the truth. Dad has been stealing money so I can be happy. The woman I'm seeing is married and her husband won't give her a divorce. He'd rather kill her than divorce her. So, we're running away.

MR. PICKLES: That's very sweet and not going to happen, Zach. That money belongs to me. I built this pier. Not literally. But I put things on it. I created a destination that would attract the bulging waistlines of tourists from all over the world. They come and pay for overpriced food while waddling through overpriced stores and attractions. And we take their pictures and make them pay more so they can remember the things I built cheaply for their amusement. There's no there here. It's all fake. We're like Vegas without the gambling. Six Flags if it only had one flag. At half-mast. We're a food court without a mall. And the people come. In droves. To drink alcohol in souvenir cups and look at the water. Tourists. Tell them it's special and they'll treat it like it's special. Tell them they just have to go and they will. And they'll come back. Why? Because they've been here before. They feed on empty traditions. Your daddy has been stealing the money I've been siphoning from all the fanny packs. You're not going anywhere. I want it back.

ZACH: I'll stop you. I have a gun. (They all freeze and then look puzzled when Zach doesn't move.) In the safe in the office.

(Zach runs back into the maze. Mr. Pickles sends Jack in to follow him. They follow the exact same path, but in reverse.)

TONY: No, son! Don't!

(Tony follows.)

MR. PICKLES: Dammit!

(Mr. Pickles follows Tony brandishing his nail file. All four of them are following the same path back. Once Zach emerges from the other side of the tunnel, he runs to the office and begins to open the combination safe. He opens it just in time to turn the gun on Jack.)

ZACH: Hold it right there.

JACK: Whoa, Zack! Whoa!

TONY: Easy, son. Don't do anything foolish.

MR. PICKLES: What'd I miss?

ZACH: I have a gun. Don't anyone move. (Zach takes a ring full of keys out of his pocket and starts looking for a key while continuing to hold the gun on Zach and Mr. Pickles.) I'm calling the shots, now.

TONY: Zach.

ZACH: Shut up, Dad. After I'm done wasting the three of you-

TONY: The three of you? Me, too?

ZACH: You, too, Dad. I'm going to cash in on your life insurance and my inheritance. I'm going to step over your lifeless bodies and grab those bank account transfers and those plane tickets and I'm going to Costa Rica with Myrna Pickles.

36

MR. PICKLES: My wife?

ZACH: Your wife!

MR. PICKLES: I'll kill her.

ZACH: We've been in love for over a year. She comes here when you're out of town and we break into the Chicago Children's Museum and make love in the ball pit.

MR. PICKLES: Ew.

ZACH: Jesus!

TONY: What are you looking for?

ZACH: The file cabinet key. I keep the bullets locked up separate from the gun. Too many kids around here to risk accidents.

TONY: It's the tiny copper one.

(Mr. Pickles smacks Jack in the arm. Jack grabs Zach's gun and points it at Zach who reacts like it's loaded.)

MR. PICKLES: It's not loaded. Look. Here's what's going to happen. You're not going to kill anyone. You're going to take Myrna and flee to Costa Rica like you planned. But no divorce. I hate divorces. Myrna would try to get even more money out of me than what this costs. Go. Be happy. Choke on your happiness.

ZACH: That's very nice of you, Mr. Pickles.

MR. PICKLES: It is. But if Myrna has found love, too, then God bless.

(Mr. Pickles and Jack hold hands.)

TONY: You were going to shoot me?

JACK: He was going to shoot all of us.

MR. PICKLES: Kids, right?

TONY: Do I still have a job?

MR. PICKLES: You do. But I'm still not going to finish that manicure.

(Blackout)

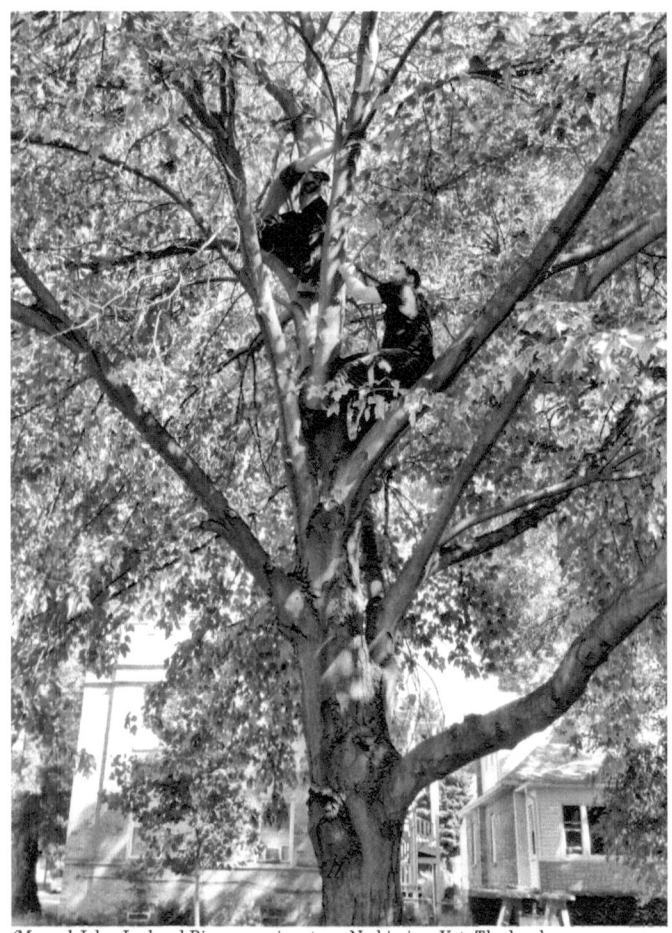

(Me and John Jughead Pierson up in a tree. No kissing. Yet. The lovely
Paige Saliba took the picture.)

38

"Johnny's Tree"
Written by Joe Janes

CAST:
Narrator
Johnny, 30s
The Wife, 30s
The Squirrel
The Bird
The Tree

(Lights up on Johnny standing in his front yard next to an oak tree.)

NARRATOR (VO): This is Johnny Foibles. Not too long ago, he took to standing in his front yard. While most of his neighbors watched the television or went to PTA meetings, Johnny stood in his front yard next to an oak tree. One day, he decided to stay there. His wife was none too pleased.

(The wife appears, presumably from the front door of their home. she is wearing an apron and stirring something in a mixing bowl)

THE WIFE: Johnny, come on in. Dinner's almost ready. (There is no response. The bowl is gone, she removes the apron) Johnny, come on in. Dinner's ready. I made your favorite. Meatloaf cakes, mashed potatoes, corn on the cob and carrots. (There is no response. She now wears a sexy housecoat, perhaps a kimono.) Johnny, come on in. I'm going to bed. A little early. (No response. She now wears a hairnet and an unflattering housecoat.) Johnny! Stop being a freak! The neighbors are watching! Get your ass inside and come to bed! (No response. We hear the sound of crickets as it gets darker. Defeated, she takes a blanket and walks over to him and drapes it around his shoulders. She places her hand on his cheek. Kisses him, but not on the lips.) What do you want, Johnny Foibles? (No response. With a little sadness, she walks inside.)

THE NARRATOR: Don't be too harsh with Johnny. He had a lot on his mind. He lost his job. A job he loved. He used to sell watches. He was very good at it. Until people stopped buying watches. Before that, he sold VCRs. And telephone directories. Before that, he tried to get out of sales by managing a record store. He could also get you a good deal on a portable cassette player for awhile. Before that, he sold typewriters door-to-door. He always loved what he was doing while he was doing it. He hated that people stopped loving to buy those things he loved to sell. He didn't know what he was going to do. He didn't know what he wanted. (Johnny stands there throughout the night. It gets even darker.) Johnny wasn't sure if he was dreaming or having some kind of divine intervention. In the middle of the night, in his darkest hour, he heard a voice whisper to him...

THE TREE: Climb me.

(Johnny's eyes widen. It becomes lighter outside. We hear the sound of birds chirping. It gets lighter. The wife comes out in her housecoat with a cup of coffee. She stands next to her husband and also looks out.)

JOHNNY: I know what I want.

THE WIFE: That's nice. What? You do? What? What is it, Johnny! Tell me!

JOHNNY: I want to climb that tree.

THE WIFE: Oh.

(Johnny doffs off his blanket and begins climbing the tree.)

THE NARRATOR: And Johnny did exactly that. He climbed the tree in his front yard.

THE WIFE: Johnny! What are you doing?

JOHNNY: I'm climbing this here tree!

THE WIFE: But why?

JOHNNY: I haven't climbed a tree since I was a kid. I used to love it. Sometime during the night, I realized I have a perfectly good tree here and it's never been climbed. By anyone. That's a shame. A shame for me and a shame for the tree. You should come join me!

THE WIFE: You should come down. I have to go to work.

JOHNNY: This is my work, now.

THE WIFE: How long are you going to stay up there?

JOHNNY: Until I find the answer.

THE WIFE: The answer to what?

JOHNNY: What I want to do with the rest of my life!

THE WIFE: Be careful. I love you. Good-bye, Johnny. (She walks back into the house as Johnny continues climbing.)

THE NARRATOR: Johnny's wife couldn't stand to see her husband this way. So she left. Never to return. Johnny reached the most tippy-toppiest branch he could reach. And he sat on a limb and he waited. And he waited. And he waited. And then a squirrel scurried up the other side of the tree and stared at him because Johnny was a most curious sight.

40

JOHNNY: Hello.

THE SQUIRREL: Hi. (Pause) You're too big for a squirrel and too featherless to be a bird.

JOHNNY: I'm Johnny.

THE SQUIRREL: And Johnnys live in trees?

JOHNNY: No. Not really. I was standing down there last night and I thought I heard this tree say, "Climb me."

THE SQUIRREL: Oh, yeah. They do that.

JOHNNY: They do?

THE SQUIRREL: Sure. That's why you see squirrels climbing trees all the time. Trees love it. Tickles their bark.

JOHNNY: Well, what do you know?

THE SQUIRREL: I don't know what I know. I do know, you stand next to a tree long enough and you'll hear it. Or feel it. They don't have lips like we do.

JOHNNY: Do you know what you want to do with your life, Mr. Squirrel?

THE SQUIRREL: It's just Squirrel. I'm not married.

JOHNNY: Do you know what you want to do with your life, Squirrel?

THE SQUIRREL: I know I want to eat and I want to play. I like tormenting dogs.

JOHNNY: Do you feel like it's what you were born to do?

THE SQUIRREL: I just know it's what I do. And I like it. Gotta go. Going to go buzz that dog walker down there. See ya', Johnny!

JOHNNY: Bye, Squirrel.

> (The Squirrel scurries away. We hear dogs barking in the background.
> Johnny smiles.)

THE NARRATOR: Johnny enjoyed his chat with Squirrel, but then realized he still didn't know what he wanted and was even less certain he'd find the answer in a tree. But he didn't give up. He waited. And he waited. And he waited some more. The daylight hours were just fading away when a bird flittered down onto one of the branches near Johnny.

JOHNNY: Hello.

THE BIRD (BRITISH): UM, YES. Greetings.

JOHNNY: Nice night.

THE BIRD: It is pleasant, so far.

JOHNNY: You're not going to ask me why I'm in a tree?

THE BIRD: No. Nothing surprises me anymore. I just assume your mother abandoned you here and you never learned to fly. In fact, that's the opinion I'm going to have of you. I will regard it as irrefutable fact.

JOHNNY: But it's not true.

THE BIRD: Yes, it is. Your lies will not sway me from the truth, orphan bird.

JOHNNY: But I'm too big to be a bird.

THE BIRD: You clearly don't know much about birds. Which is what I would expect from a bird that has spent his life stuck in the same tree without parental tutelage.

JOHNNY: But I walk on two legs and don't fly.

THE BIRD: So, you're an ostrich. What do you want from me?

JOHNNY: I want you to tell me what I want to do with my life?

THE BIRD: I can't do that. I'm not an ostrich.

JOHNNY: Well, tell me what you want to do with your life.

THE BIRD: I want to continue doing what I do. Eat, fly, poop on things.

JOHNNY: Do you poop on people?

THE BIRD: Only for sport. I consider automobiles to be my art. Eat some berries and hit a white jaguar in motion and you've got a Jackson Pollack.

JOHNNY: I don't know who that is.

THE BIRD: You really need to get out of this tree. Go poop on a museum.

JOHNNY: But the tree told me to climb it.

THE BIRD: Trees lie, too. Probably playing a joke on you. They don't poop so they have to find other forms of entertainment. I have to go. Looks like a storm's coming. Great for getting worms after. Dreadful while it's going on. See you, Ostrich.

JOHNNY: Bye, bird.

(The sky turns ominously dark and a serious storm begins.)

THE NARRATOR: And storm it did. Johnny held on for dear life as he was pelted by heavy rains and stinging hail. And he would have made it to morning clinging to that old oak tree if it weren't for the lightning.

(We hear a crack of lightning that strikes the tree in a bright flash and propels Johnny to the ground.)

THE NARRATOR: Johnny fell 25 feet all the way to the ground where he landed on his back with a plop. And while he lay there, the rain stopped. Morning came. Squirrel interrupted eating a tomato to notice his friend. (We see Squirrel regarding Johnny from a distance) The clouds parted and a ray of light shined on him. Johnny knew. Johnny Foibles finally knew what he wanted.

JOHNNY: I want... (The Squirrel pricks up his ears.) An ambulance. (The Squirrel goes back to eating a nut.)

THE NARRATOR: There's a lesson to our story and it is this. Some lessons can only be learned while sitting in a tree. This is not one of them.

(Johnny wipes off his eye.)

JOHNNY: A bird just pooped in my eye.

(Blackout.)

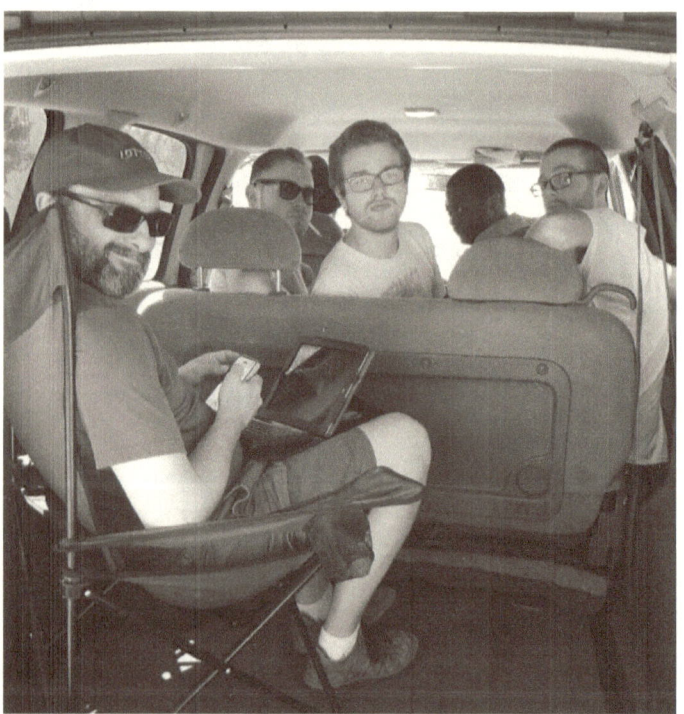

(Todd McNeely's van. Me, Jared Popkin, Ryan Hake, Jared Michael Grant and J. Cody Spelman. Todd's driving. Ricki Staffieri took the pic. This one was done just as a hoot. Todd suggested driving me around in crowded downtown traffic while he chainsmoked. This was one of the few where the entire cast and director were able to join me. We were packed in. I had second thoughts about it until Todd did an inspired thing. He turned on to Lower Wacker Drive which is like a whole other underground city. We got lost and ended up on a construction site. Todd hit a pothole hard. I felt it in my teeth. We broke his van. He had to drive back to Indiana stopping every 20 minutes to refill the leaking radiator with water. Thanks for the sacrifice, Todd.)

"Todd's 1999 Mercury Villager, Lower Wacker"
Written by Joe Janes

CAST:
Todd, 20s
Ricky, 20s
Rye, 30s
Jared, 30s

(Lights up on Todd and Ricky driving in Todd's 1999 Mercury Villager.
They are both very clean cut looking. Think college prep. Todd is driving.)

RICKY: Thanks for taking me along, Todd.

RICKY: Thanks for being someone I can trust, Ricky.

RICKY: You really enjoy this.

TODD: Honestly, I feel like I'm doing God's work. Helping to give people
who have lost their way some dignity. Give them a chance.

RICKY: I've never been down here before.

TODD: Lower Wacker is the best place to look for fallen angels.

RICKY: It's like a whole different world down here.

TODD: A lot of little side pockets and alcoves. Plenty of places for someone
who's homeless to set up with a cardboard box and a blanket.

RICKY: That's so sad. No one should live like that.

TODD: That's why we're here. To try to make a difference.

(Todd stops the van.)

RICKY: We're stopping?

TODD: Yeah. The good thing about all the construction is that it creates
these little areas where it's easy to park at night.

RICKY: I thought we drove around until we saw someone.

TODD: No need to. We can let them come to us. Which they will. Wait and
see. We represent an opportunity to them. We're living examples of a better
life.

(They sit and wait for a moment.)

RICKY: It's really quiet down here.

TODD: No one likes to drive down here, if they can avoid it. Especially during summer construction. It's a bad place to risk breaking down... Bingo.

(Jared enters from the house. He is homeless.)

JARED: You lost?

(Todd rolls down his window.)

TODD: I believe the question is, "Are you lost?"

JARED: If you have some change you can spare, I'd be much obliged. I can do without you trying to spread the word of your Lord over this way.

(Todd gets out of the van and opens up the side door.)

TODD: We're just here to help, brother. We have some food, if you want it. (Todd reaches in and pulls out a brown lunch sack. Jared approaches cautiously.) You can have some if you like. It's a ham sandwich. Some chips. A cookie.

(He holds it out to Jared. Jared takes it and looks inside it.)

JARED: Thanks. Sorry to be so suspicious. Hi.

RICKY: Hello.

JARED: Do you have more?

TODD: Yes, but...

JARED: It's not for me. Hey, Rye!

(Rye comes out from the shadows. A very shy homeless man with a Band-Aid on his chin.)

JARED: It's okay. They brought food.

(Todd holds out another bag for Rye. Rye gets closer. Ricky opens his passenger door and spooks Rye. Jared grabs Rye.)

JARED: It's okay! It's okay! (To Ricky) You scared him!

RICKY: I'm sorry. I am so sorry. I didn't mean anything. Is he going to be all right?

JARED: Look at me. Look at me. (Rye does.) We good? You cool?

(Rye nods. Jared takes the bag from Todd and hands it to Rye who starts to nibble from it like a small animal.)

RYE: You guys from a church or something?

TODD: We like to help.

RICKY: We're helpers. Todd's been doing this for a while. It's my first time. How long have you guys been homeless?

JARED: A long time.

RICKY: Why don't you go somewhere warmer?

JARED: What? I don't know. You offering a ride to Florida?

TODD: He's just curious. He doesn't mean anything by it.

RICKY: You could walk. Start walking before it gets cold, by the time winter hits you'll be sleeping on a beach. If I were homeless, I'd start walking south.

RYE: You'd be dead by the time you left the state. That's a lot of walking without food or water or shelter.

JARED: And small towns aren't so friendly to panhandlers.

RYE: It's hard enough to get food during the day in a busy city.

JARED: Not too many farmers going to let you sleep with their daughter when you smell like a sewer rat. Right, Rye?

RYE: That's right.

RICKY: I thought you guys rode the rails. You could take trains all the way there. Sing songs.

JARED: We're not hobos.

RICKY: What's the difference?

TODD: Ricky, hobos are homeless because they want to be. They're people who have chosen to live that lifestyle.

RYE: I did not choose to live on the street.

JARED: Neither of us did. Rye got booted out of a mental health home when their funding got cut.

47

RYE: I have family. In another state. I'm sure they worry about me.

JARED: I got kicked out of the army.

TODD: Why did you get kicked out of the army?

JARED: Apparently, I like killing too much.

RICKY: You seem pretty smart. Got all your limbs. Can't you get a job at McDonald's or something?

JARED: I did. Got let go when I pressed the manager's face onto the grill while breaking his fingers.

RYE: He has anger issues.

JARED: Look, you want to help the homeless, let me give you a tip. Don't ask so many damn questions. Just help.

RICKY: Hey...

TODD: He's right.

RICKY: I'm sorry. I didn't mean to be rude. Do you want to...?

TODD: No. You do it. It's your first time. Go ahead.

RICKY: Let me ask you just one more teeny tiny question.

JARED: What?

RICKY: Do you want to make fifty bucks?

JARED: What?

RYE: Yes?

(Todd takes out his cell phone and starts recording.)

TODD: We want to put a little video on the Internet.

JARED: You guys are sick fucks.

RICKY: All you have to do is try to punch each other's lights out.

TODD: You don't expect us to give you money for free, do you? This is a job offer.

48

JARED: You sick fucks need to get back in your mom's van- (Rye sucker punches him.) What the fuck, Rye?

RYE: I want the fifty bucks! Fifty bucks and I can get a bus ticket. See my parents.

JARED: Your parents don't want you, fool.

RYE: Maybe they do. Maybe they changed their minds.

JARED: And if they don't, you're fucked. Stuck in Salt Lake.

(Rye throws another punch, but Jared is expecting it and grabs Rye and holds him in a half nelson.)

JARED: Knock it the fuck off, Rye.

RICKY: Hey, Rye. Beat the shit out of him and the money's yours.

TODD: Yeah. Beat the shit out of him. He's kind of an asshole.

JARED: You guys shut the fuck up or I'll shove my fists down your throats.

TODD: You can try. (While still recording, Todd pulls a crowbar or tire iron out of the back of the van.)

RICKY: We're just two guys trying to help the homeless.

TODD: The police will understand.

RICKY: We gave you food. Offered you money. You turn on us, well, (He takes a knife out of his pocket and opens it up) that just makes a better video.

RYE: I want that fucking money. I want that fucking money, Jared.

JARED: And you're willing to do what these jag holes say just to get it?

RYE: Yes! I've done worse. I want to go home!

JARED: Show us the money!

TODD: We're good for it.

JARED: Show us or I drag him out of here and you don't get your rocks off on a hobo fight.

(Ricky reaches into his pocket and pulls out a fifty-dollar bill.)

49

RICKY: Right here, Hobo Joe. Happy? But only the winner gets the money.

JARED: Okay, Rye. Look at me. We'll fight. And you get the money no matter what. Okay?

RYE: I'm going to beat the shit out of you.

JARED: I doubt that.

TODD: This is so awesome.

(Jared releases Rye and pushes him away a few steps. Rye recovers himself. Jared and Rye face off, circle each other a bit, like boxers.)

JARED: What do you guys do? Take these home and jerk off to them?

RICKY: You wish.

TODD: We're not perverts. We just enjoy giving to charity. And seeing two homeless dudes fuck themselves up for chump change.

RICKY: It's a perfectly good business transaction for you.

(Jared steps in and hits Rye on the jaw. He goes down. Out cold. Jared grabs the money, but Ricky holds on to it tight. Ricky stabs Jared. He is surprised that he has done this. This pisses Jared off. He beats the ever-living shit out of Ricky. Todd keeps recording until Ricky is out on the ground. Jared turns to look at Todd. Todd, who sees the look in his phone, freaks out, drops the crowbar and bolts on foot. Jared, holding his side where he was stabbed, picks up the fifty bucks and takes Rye and puts him in the van. Jared gets in the drivers seat.)

RYE: Are we going to Salt Lake?

JARED: I don't think we can make to Salt Lake. Or to Florida. We've got fifty bucks. A stolen van with half a tank of gas. I'm bleeding. I may have just killed a guy. All we can do is go as far as we can and see what happens.

(He starts the van, begins driving, lights fade to black.)

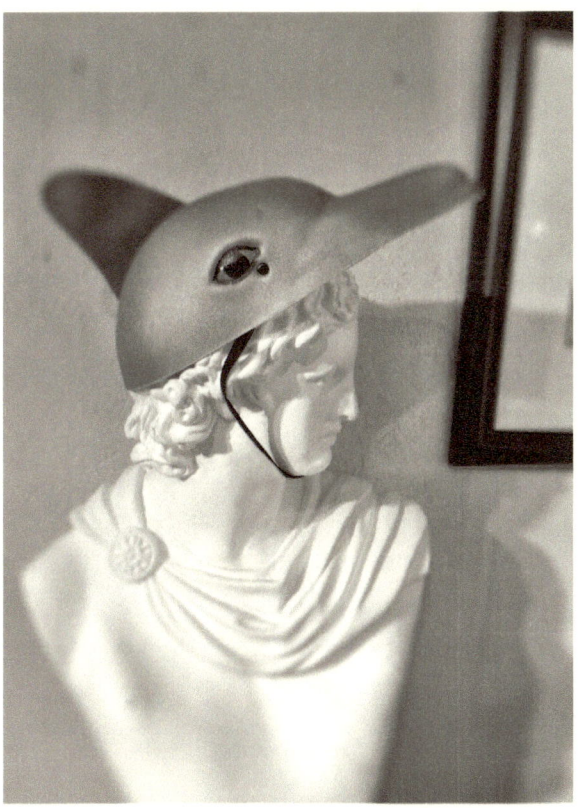

(Dolphin Encounter was written in between *50 Plays* and *Seven Deadly Plays* for Robot vs. Dinosaur's *Pretty From A Distance.* It was first performed in a preview at Chicago's *Sketchfest* at Stage773.)

"Dolphin Encounter"
Written by Joe Janes

CAST:
Captain Billy, 50s
Mitch, 30s
Dolphin

(Lights up on Captain Billy sitting in a lawn chair. He wears shades and sits very still. Mitch walks up to him. Mitch wears a long-sleeve CSNY t-shirt.)

MITCH: Hello?

(Nothing happens.)

MITCH: Are you Captain Billy? The guy at the bait shop said you were Captain Billy.

CAPTAIN BILLY (not moving): I'm Captain Billy. (Captain Billy removes his shades and looks at Mitch.) You Mitch?

MITCH: I have a gift certificate. (He hands it to Captain Billy.)

CAPTAIN BILLY: That's great.

MITCH: My aunt gave it to me for my birthday.

CAPTAIN BILLY: Happy birthday.

MITCH: It was three months ago.

CAPTAIN BILLY: I take it back, then. You ready to go?

MITCH: Um...where's the dolphin?

CAPTAIN BILLY: Right down there. (He points down off the edge of the dock. Mitch peers over and takes a look.)

MITCH: I don't see anything.

CAPTAIN BILLY: He's down there. The water's a little murky, today. Pollution.

MITCH: Oh. Is it safe?

CAPTAIN BILLY: Hasn't killed anyone, yet.

MITCH: Is it safe for the dolphin?

52

CAPTAIN BILLY: Oh, sure. He's a dolphin. They're tough. They have blowholes. You ready to do this?

MITCH: Yes. I've always wanted to swim with a dolphin.

CAPTAIN BILLY: Not really a swimming thing. That's why it's called Captain Billy's Dolphin Encounter. Not allowed to call it swimming anymore. Not since the lawsuit. Not a lot of room down there. More of a treading water, hanging out thing. It's a lot like swimming. You're both in the water.

MITCH: Well, okay.

CAPTAIN BILLY: Going like that or did you bring trunks?

MITCH: I have trunks. Where can I change?

CAPTAIN BILLY: Right here, I guess. Most people come already trunked up. There are people around.

MITCH: Maybe I can-

CAPTAIN BILLY: The bait shop won't let you use their bathroom. Homeless people. They ruined it for everyone.

MITCH: I guess I can use my car...

CAPTAIN BILLY: People will think you're a perv. Especially with the all the kids around. Here. Tell you what. (He gets up and unfurls the towel he's been sitting on.) Change behind this.

MITCH: People will still see behind me.

CAPTAIN BILLY: Point it toward the ocean. The dolphin doesn't care. Look, Mitch, I have a doctor's appoiintment. The sooner you get into your trunks and into the pen, the more time you'll have with the dolphin.

              (Mitch starts to change out of his clothes behind the towel.)

MITCH: Does the dolphin have a name?

CAPTAIN BILLY: Dolphin.

MITCH: You didn't give him a name?

CAPTAIN BILLY: Dolphins are one of the smartest animals on the planet. They don't like cute names. They resent it.

MITCH: I'm going to leave my t-shirt on.

CAPTAIN BILLY: Neither the dolphin nor I care about your man teats. (He puts the towel away.) I'll keep an eye on your stuff. Here's some goggles and a snorkel. (Mitch puts them on.) You look great. Just step over the edge when you're ready.

(Mitch walks to the edge of the dock.)

MITCH: Here I go.

CAPTAIN BILLY: Enjoy your dolphin encounter.

(Captain Billy pushes him on the back and Mitch falls forward into the water. We now are under water with Mitch. He is semi-treading water looking for the dolphin. He thinks he sees it and swims over to it. The dolphin is just standing there. He turns and stares at Mitch. They do this for a moment. Mitch attempts to say "hello" with the snorkel in his mouth.)

DOLPHIN: Hi.

(Mitch attempts to say something but it's unintelligible.)

DOLPHIN: Take the thingy out of your mouth.

(Mitch does.)

MITCH: You can understand me.

DOLPHIN: "Hello" was pretty easy to figure out.

MITCH: You're a very smart dolphin.

DOLPHIN: Don't patronize me. If I were smart, I wouldn't be stuck in this tank.

MITCH: You don't like this.

DOLPHIN: I can promise it's more of a thrill for you than me. Nothing personal.

MITCH: None taken. Well, it's nice to meet you. My name's Mitch.

DOLPHIN: Hi, Mitch. I'm Frank.

MITCH: Captain Billy said you didn't have a name.

FRANK: Captain Billy never asked.

54

MITCH: He just calls you Dolphin.

DOLPHIN: I answer to that, too. Someone shouts dolphin around here, they're probably talking about me. Know what I mean, Human?

MITCH: You really are super smart.

DOLPHIN: I'm not. Pretty average. There's a lot I don't know. I don't know how to drive a car.

MITCH: But you know what a car is.

DOLPHIN: You're easy to impress. Hey, Crosby, Stills, Nash and Young. I know that guy. (He points to Mitch's t-shirt.)

MITCH: What guy?

DOLPHIN: Whatz-his-name. David Crosby. He came here once.

MITCH: David Crosby likes dolphins?

DOLPHIN: Hard to say. Nice guy, but he was pretty stoned. That might have been my last fun day. He was touching everything. Oh, David Crosby.

MITCH: So, it's okay if people touch you.

DOLPHIN: Most people just want to get near me. Some touch my fin. Or, if you're David Crosby, you lick it hoping it will get you higher.

MITCH: He did that?

DOLPHIN: Well, I may have told him it might work. (He winks.) Some folks want me to nuzzle them with my nose. Tell them if they have cancer.

MITCH: You can do that?

DOLPHIN: No. Just another "smart dolphin" rumor run amok. Some dolphin gets pissed at a picture taking douchebag and thumps him in the chest a few times, guy turns out to have lung cancer, everyone thinks the dolphin's a genius. You humans.

CAPTAIN BILLY (off): Hey, Mitch! Hurry up! I have to go get my balls checked.

MITCH: Well, it was nice meeting you Frank.

DOLPHIN: You, too, Mitch.

MITCH: You're not happy doing this, are you?

DOLPHIN: I'm miserable.

MITCH: I'm sorry.

DOLPHIN: Not your fault.

MITCH: Is there anything I can do?

DOLPHIN: Toss a loaded handgun down here, sometime. Wouldn't mind putting a lateral blowhole through my temples.

MITCH: I don't think I could do that.

DOLPHIN: If you really felt sorry for me, you wouldn't think twice.

MITCH: My aunt keeps the gun locked up. She doesn't trust me around firearms.

DOLPHIN: Smart woman. (Pause) So, Mitch. Do you want me to nuzzle you or something?

MITCH: Only if you want to.

(Dolphin walks over to Mitch and rubs his nose against Mitch's shoulder. Mitch gives him a hug.)

MITCH: Thanks, Frank.

DOLPHIN: You're welcome. (Dolphin struggles to speak.)Your hand is on my blowhole. Press harder. (Mitch removes his hand and Franks gasps.) So close.

(Mitch starts to swim away.)

DOLPHIN: Hey, Mitch. Come back and visit some time. Most people come down here and they're all grabby and squealy. You treated me with respect. I appreciate that.

(Mitch is about to exit. He stops and looks at Dolphin. He takes off his CSNY t-shirt and tosses it to Dolphin. Mitch exits. Dolphin stands on a small rock and takes one of the sleeves and attaches it to a hook hanging off the dock. He then puts the other sleeve around his neck. Lights fade.)

56

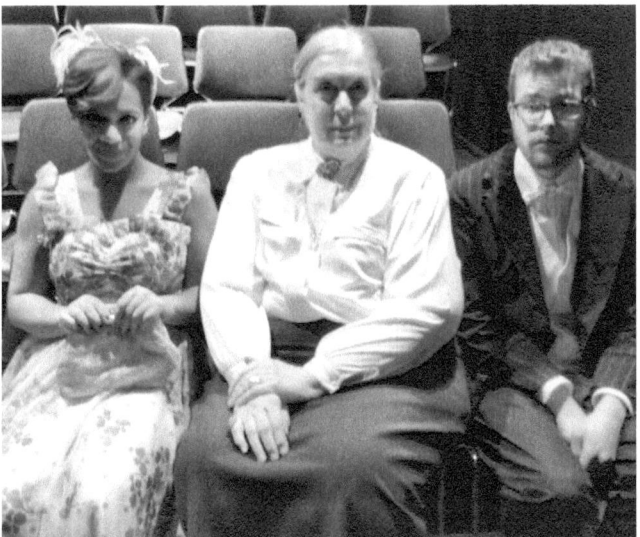

(Sasha Smith, Kathleen Perkins and Ryan Hake in my piece for 2011's
Columbia College's New Plays Festival. This is a 24-Hour play fest put on
by the theatre department organized by the wonderful and amazing
Stephanie Shaw. I love doing these. I never know what I'm going to write. A
big inspiration was director Tom Mula telling me he loved old horror movies
from the 30s and 40s and we both are crazy for James Wale's *The Old Dark
House*. The title comes from a saying written on a lady's tote bag that I saw
on the El train on the way home to write the script. The bag said "There Is
Thunder In Our Hearts". I have no idea what it is in reference to.)

"There Is A Thunder In Our Hearts"
Written by Joe Janes

CAST
Azalea Mintz, 60s
Morgan, 20s
Miss Lillian Bond, 20s

(In the dark, we hear a cold wind blowing through the corridors of an old, large house. There is a crack of thunder and a flash of lightening. In the lightening, we see Azalea Mintz standing far upstage right. Her face is twisted and defiant. Another flash of lightening finds her throwing her head back and laughing. In the dark, the sounds subside and lights gently come up on two wingback chairs flanking an antique table. Azalea is now seated, looking calm and ladylike. Downstage left, hanging from the ceiling, is a beat up stuffed teddy bear hanging from a rope. The rope comes almost all the way to the floor. On the floor, under the bear, is a small child's chair knocked over and a piece of paper. We hear a grand doorbell peal. There are a few moments of silence as Azalea sits up just slightly. We hear it, again.)

AZALEA: Morgan! The door!

(Morgan the butler, in a classic butler uniform, enters stage left and moves across the parlor behind Azalea towards the door. He stops for a moment and sees the teddy bear. He is slightly stunned and then saddened. He composes himself and continues offstage to the door.)

MORGAN (offstage): May I help you?

LILLIAN (offstage): Yes. How do you do? My name is Miss Lillian Bond-

AZALEA (shouting): Entrez vous!

(Morgan steps back into the parlor.)

MORGAN: Madam?

AZALEA: Entrez vous, Morgan. Entrez vous!

MORGAN: Yes, Madam. (He exits and we hear him offstage.) Right this way. (Morgan re-enters with Lillian showing her into the parlor. Lillian wears a lovely white dress.) Miss Lillian Bond to see Madam Azalea Mintz.

(Azalea presents her hand, but does not get out of her chair.)

AZALEA: How do you do, Lillian? It is so lovely to see you and you look delicious.

(Lillian approaches and takes Azalea's hand with a slight curtsey.)

LILLIAN: Thank you. So do you, Azalea.

(Azalea gestures for her to sit and she does.)

AZALEA: That was quite a storm we had last night, wasn't it?

LILLIAN: It sure packed a wallop.

AZALEA: The clouds are still look dark and foreboding. I fear we might be in store for another storm soon.

LILLIAN: This is such a lovely (she sees the teddy bear) home...that you...have.

AZALEA: Teddy was despondent. To be honest, we should have seen it coming. Morgan. Tea.

MORGAN (choking back tears): Yes, Madam.

(He exits.)

AZALEA: Let us, then, discuss business.

LILLIAN: Um. Yes. Let's. We are prepared to make you a very generous offer on your house.

AZALEA: I am ready to accept it.

LILLIAN: Oh. Well. That was easy. Are you sure you don't want to know how much...?

AZALEA: You said generous. I assume it's generous. Unless you lied.

LILLIAN: I can assure you I did not lie. Here. (She reaches into her small purse and pulls out a small piece of paper and small pencil.) Let me write down the figure. (She does and passes it to Azalea. Azalea reads it.)

AZALEA: You could have said that out loud.

LILLIAN: I'm just trying to be discreet.

(Azalea puts the piece of paper down on the table.)

AZALEA: It's more than I expected. Très généreux.

LILLIAN: Oui. Good for you, I suppose.

AZALEA: Good for me. Hooray!

LILLIAN: Hooray!

(Morgan enters backwards with tea service. He is trying not to look at the teddy bear. He pours them tea.)

AZALEA: Thank you, Morgan.

(Morgan picks up the piece of paper and reads it. He looks incredulously at both the women.)

AZALEA: Thank you, Morgan.

(Weeping, Morgan exits.)

AZALEA: Don't judge Morgan too harshly. He's a good man. He was born in this house. Has seldom stepped foot off the property. His father was also my butler. He has known no other life. I schooled him in my spare time. I taught him French. Teddy was his best friend. In the end, there was nothing he could do. When someone decides it's time to go, it's time to go.

LILLIAN: Did he leave a note?

AZALEA: Yes. It simply read, "Je suis perdu." I am lost.

LILLIAN (reluctantly sipping tea): Losing one's best friend is difficult.

AZALEA: So is losing one's home. What will you do with this old pile of timber and bones?

LILLIAN: We're going to tear it down.

AZALEA: Oh?

LILLIAN: We're going to build several condominiums and there will be shops along the first floor. Tea shops. Dress shops. A haberdashery. Perhaps a small grocer.

AZALEA: I once knew a small grocer. He courted me. Nice fellow. Horrible kisser. Insisted on always using his tongue. It felt like a baby snake trying to slither down my throat.

LILLIAN: Oh, that's awful. Did you tell him? How could you?

AZALEA: I couldn't tell him. So, I bit it off. He got the message.

(Morgan re-enters. He is still upset. Very tense. He has a small plate of cookies he sets on the table.)

MORGAN: Excuse me, Madam Mintz. These are some almond sugar cookies I baked especially for you. And your guest. I hope you like them. Please try them. Please try them by picking one up and putting it in your mouth and chewing.

(Azalea and Lillian slowly go ahead and follow his directions, afraid he might snap.)

LILLIAN: Oh, these are scrumptious.

AZALEA: Morgan is a whiz in the kitchen.

MORGAN: These will be the last cookies of mine you will taste Miss Lillian Bond and Madam Azalea Mintz. The last and final morsel of cookiness. For I am leaving.

AZALEA: Morgan. You cannot leave. Not yet. Who will rub soothing ointment into my bunions?

MORGAN: My best friend is dead and you have sold my home out from under me.

AZALEA: But that won't be for some time, right? These things take time.

LILLIAN: Actually, we need you out in two weeks.

AZALEA: Oh, dear.

MORGAN: Time to celebrate! (To Azalea) Have another cookie! Eat it! Eat it! Eat it! (She does.) You have one, too. (Lillian takes another cookie, but does not eat it.)

LILLIAN: Thank you, Morgan. You know, you can probably find employment in a bakeshop.

MORGAN: Of course, I could. I'm not incompetent.

AZALEA: There's no need for this tone, Morgan.

MORGAN: Do you know the kind of woman you are doing business with, Miss Bond? Does it even matter to you?

LILLIAN: Miss Mintz is a well-respected member of society. She gives to charity.

AZALEA(to the audience): I give to charity.

MORGAN: She drove Teddy to suicide! Her constant haranguing. Her constant and complete unsatisfaction at everything Teddy ever did or was. He tried. He tried so hard. I even told him last night, "Teddy. Don't worry. Some day, we'll leave this musky prison of talcum powder and wood polish. We'll run away and frolic in the woods. You can be among your own kind. We'll laugh. We'll play. We'll eat cookies. We'll be free. No more haranguing." And that was the last time I saw Teddy smile.

AZALEA: He's not smiling, now.

MORGAN: Because you got to him. You got to him, somehow. Cold, heartless sow.

AZALEA: Say it in French!

MORGAN: Je ne vais jamais parler français, encore une fois!

AZALEA: How dare you!

MORGAN: You won't even let me take him down.

AZALEA: He stays until the lesson is learned.

LILLIAN: How can Teddy- he's just a-?

AZALEA: Morgan needs to learn the lesson.

MORGAN: And what lesson is that? Not to listen to the venomous words that drip out of your mouth?

AZALEA: That I'm your best friend, Morgan. Not Teddy! I am! I'm your best friend. A mommy is always a boy's best friend. (She grabs her stomach.) OH, my.

LILLIAN: Are you okay?

AZALEA: I don't feel so good.

LILLIAN: Morgan, call a physician!

MORGAN: It's too late.

LILLIAN: If you won't, I will – (She gets up, but feels a shock of pain in her stomach that sits her back down.)

MORGAN: I have laced the cookies with arsenic. (To Lillian) You will likely survive.

62

AZALEA: Thank goodness.

MORGAN (To Azalea): You most certainly will not. I have been poisoning your cookies for years. You have enough arsenic in you to take down three elephants.

AZALEA: You are a fool, Morgan. A fool.

MORGAN (To Lillian): Even in the throes of death, harangue.

AZALEA: I was going to take care of you. What will you do, now? You are a murderer. You will go to prison. They will give you the guillotine. (To Lillian) Give all the money for the house to charity. Give it all to the orphans.

LILLIAN: It's not over, yet, Azalea. Maybe if you tried to vomit.

AZALEA: Oh, I could never do that. I have too many nice things. (She goes silent and Lillian and Morgan stare at her.) Pourquoi vous, en pleurant? Avez-vous vous imaginer que j'ai été immortel?(She dies. For a moment. Then has a spasm. Now, she's dead. Nope. One more spasm and she keels over) Merde. (She hangs over the side of the chair.)

(Morgan hangs his head down. Lillian forces herself to get up and moves over to him. She plants a big kiss on him.)

LILLIAN: Good job, Morgan. The house is now ours. We'll make a fortune. Oh, I better sit back down. (Morgan helps her sit back down.) Can't believe I took one for the team like that. (As she continues talking, he walks over to Teddy. He reads the note.) We'll tear this place down as soon as I can arrange an estate sale. Between the sale of this place and the condos, I – we'll, be millionaires. You'll be able to have your own butler. Did she say she was your mommy? What are you doing? Morgan. (Morgan unties Teddy and cradles him) That's just an old child's toy. Made of rags and stuffing. We couldn't get a penny for it. Throw it in the dustbin. (He walks back towards the kitchen.) Do you have anything for my stomach?

(Morgan turns.)

MORGAN: I'll make more cookies.

(This registers with Lillian as there is a crack of thunder and lightning. The lights go out as he walks off. Blackout and wind blowing through an old house.)

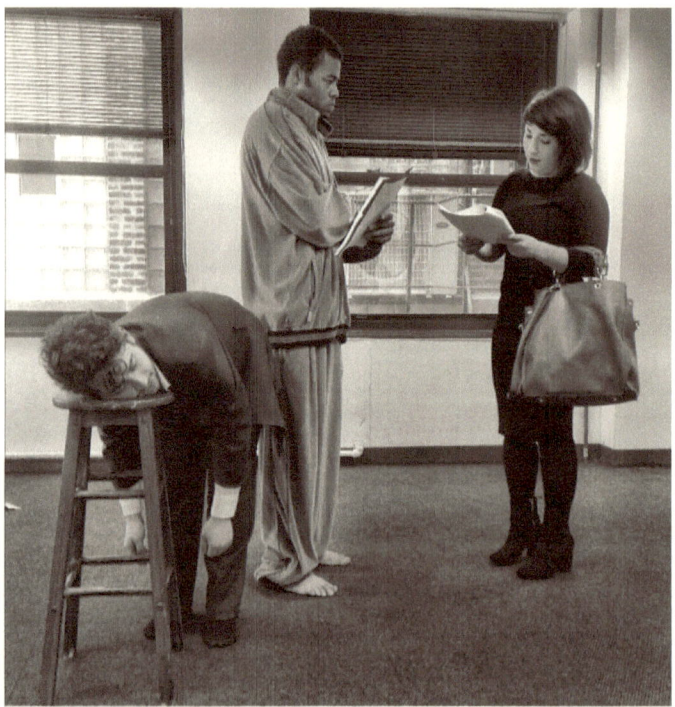

(David Gordezky, Terrence Cary and Kate Hyatt rehearsing "Couch World" for another Columbia College New Plays Festival. The inspiration for this came from organizer Stephanie Shaw's warning to the writers not to go crazy on props and set. She specifically said "Don't set your play in Couch World." I couldn't resist. And when David and Terrence mentioned they owned the outfits you see above, well, I had to make sure they were in the piece.)

"Couch World"
Written by Joe Janes

Cast
Dan, 30s
Richard, 30s
Amelia, 30s

(Lights up on Couch World. There are no couches in Couch World. There is a tall wooden stool. On the stool is a large three-ring binder filled with pages. On the spine of the binder, in magic marker, it says "Couch World." Lying on the floor on a throw rug using another rug for a blanket are Richard and Dan. Not far from them on the floor is an alarm clock. Dan and Richard are spooning, but not in a romantic way. More like in a Laurel and Hardy or Three Stooges this-is-just-how-we-sleep-way. Dan wears a zoot suit. Richard is in a crushed velvet jump suit. Richard moves his leg, much like a dog might while sleeping. He even has some slight whimpers like a sleeping dog. Without waking, Dan reaches up and scratches his ear. Richard calms down. They settle back in to a deep sleep. The alarm clock goes off. Dan pulls out from under the blanket a large mallet and whacks the clock. He falls back asleep. The alarm rings, again. Dan whacks it twice and goes back to sleep. He opens one eye and looks at the remains of the clock. He sits up a bit and looks at it full on with great suspicion. It rings again and he quickly beats the crap out of it. He sits, exhausted, but victorious. Richard sits bolt upright.)

RICHARD: It's Tuesday!

DAN: Yeah. It's Tuesday. Tuesday! It's Tuesday!

(They jump up. Richard rolls up the rugs with the mallet and clock remains in them. Dan primps, smoothing out his suit. When Richard is done, he turns to Dan. Dan strikes a pose. Richard gives him thumbs up. Dan walks over to a door and turns a sign around so that it says, "Open." He and Richard then stand facing the door and strike a pose, waiting for a customer. Any customer. They stand there for a very long time. Richard begins to slump. Dan nudges him back to attention.)

RICHARD: I could sure use a breakfast burrito. Or tamale.

DAN: We don't want to miss a customer.

(They reposition themselves. A few moments pass and Richard begins to falls asleep where he's standing. Dan does, too. Richard snaps awake.)

RICHARD: I could go and bring the food back.

DAN: There might be a rush.

(They start to fall asleep, again, and begin to use one another to lean against as they fall back asleep. A bell rings as the door opens and Amelia enters carrying a flyer on an orange piece of paper. Dan screams like a ninja. Well, a loud ninja. Ready to attack. Richard falls to the ground having lost what was holding him up. Amelia is startled and yelps.)

DAN: Oh! Oh! Oh! I'm so sorry. Come in. Come in.

(He leads her into the room.)

AMELIA: Is this Couch World?

(Richard jumps up to also help.)

RICHARD: Welcome to Couch World!

DAN: Yes. This is Couch World. Where all your dreams come true.

AMELIA: It says that on your flyer. "Couch World. Where All Your Dreams Come True. Sale This Tuesday. Open Early at 10am."

RICHARD: She got the flyer.

DAN: Of course she got the flyer. Everyone got that flyer. We printed up a lot of them.

RICHARD: Hundreds.

DAN: A few hundred. About a hundred. They're expensive.

AMELIA: It was slid under my door.

DAN: That was my idea.

AMELIA: I live in a secured high-rise condominium.

RICHARD: That was my idea.

AMELIA: What you did was not legal. It's trespassing.

DAN: It really was his idea.

AMELIA: You don't remember me, do you, Dan?

DAN: How could I forget such a pretty faceohmyGod!

RICHARD: Amelia!

(Dan gets down on his knees.)

66

DAN: Amelia! You, you, you look amazing.

AMELIA: I know I do.

DAN: Your hair. Your everything. And you've come back.

RICHARD: Oh, no, she didn't. (He takes the flyer) You just turn around and walk out that door, Amelia.

DAN: No, Richard.

RICHARD: Dan. Walk away. Walk away.

(Dan walks away to the other side of the stage.)

AMELIA: So, the little dog still barks.

RICHARD: Yeah. I bark. And I bite. I also will poop on your floors.

DAN: I can handle this.

RICHARD (gesturing for Dan to hold off): You can't just waltz in here after five years and do your womanly things and just expect Dan to drop everything and get back together with you. You broke his heart.

DAN: That is accurate.

AMELIA: Dan. I'm sorry.

DAN: You're sorry?

AMELIA: I'm sorry that's not what I'm here to do. I don't want your heart. I want... a couch.

RICHARD: A couch?

AMELIA: Yes. A couch. I saw the flyer. Thought it might be you.

DAN: How did you know it was me?

AMELIA: All of your businesses have had the same slogan. "Tapioca World – Where All Your Dreams Come True. Notary Public World – Where All Your Dreams Come True. Fax Machine World – Where All Your Dreams Come True.

RICHARD: If it ain't broke, don't fix it.

AMELIA: Are you sure it ain't broke?

DAN: No, no. That was his idea for a slogan.

RICHARD: "Couch World. If It Ain't Broke, Don't Fix it." His is better.

DAN: Mine is better.

AMELIA: I do have one question though.

DAN: I'm still single.

AMELIA: I meant... Thank you... I meant I have two questions. Why are there no couches in Couch World?

RICHARD: But there are. Hundreds.

DAN: Thousands.

RICHARD: They're all right here. (He picks up the binder. He leafs through it.) Sleeper sofas, papasan chairs, futons, sectionals-

DAN: Having our inventory all in a binder saves on overhead.

RICHARD: -micro-fiber, macro-fiber, leather, pleather.

DAN: You pick the one you want, we can have it delivered to you by the end of the day. Or by the next morning. It's cheaper if we do it in the middle of the night. If you're looking to save. Oh, look. This one is from our celebrity line. It's called The Nipsey Russell.

AMELIA: I don't know who that is.

RICHARD: None of us do.

DAN: But I do know, the man knows couches. Or knew. He might be dead. This one's the Wilford Brimley-

AMELIA: Dan.

DAN: Yes, Amelia.

AMELIA: I'm married.

DAN: Oh.

AMELIA: For five years, now.

DAN: I see.

RICHARD: We never heard from you since the night you snuck out. We woke up and all your things were gone.

AMELIA: All my things? My sleeping mat and the coffee can I used to keep my personal effects in?

RICHARD: It was our coffee can.

AMELIA: I couldn't go on living that way. Day-to-day. Not knowing if we were going to eat or not. I really did need to go out and make my own dreams come true.

DAN: Because they weren't coming true with me.

AMELIA: No. They weren't.

DAN: Dan World. Where Dreams Don't Come True.

AMELIA: It's just not the life for me, Dan. It never could be. But, you two. You seem to be doing...fine.

RICHARD: We're doing great.

DAN: I think I've finally hit upon the right formula. Couches seem to be my real calling.

RICHARD: They really are.

DAN: I don't know why I didn't see it before. I love couches. Always have. I love sitting on them. I love them almost as much as I love notarizing. Which I still do, if you...?

AMELIA: I'm good. You seem to be doing well.

RICHARD: Oh, we are.

DAN: We make enough.

RICHARD: Enough to eat and buy alarm clocks.

AMELIA: Of course you do.

DAN: We go through a lot of alarm clocks.

RICHARD: Our dreams have come true.

DAN: I have trouble sleeping. And waking.

AMELIA: Well, I guess... I didn't come to hurt you, Dan.

RICHARD: He's not hurt.

DAN: I am a little.

AMELIA: I guess I just wanted closure. And to see you, again. I did love you.

DAN: Yeah. I know. Thanks for stopping by.

(She's about to leave.)

AMELIA: I still could use a couch. We have this third bedroom that I just don't know what to do with.

DAN: You could fill it with couches.

AMELIA: Yes. Maybe I could. Let's take a look... Dan? Dan, is there one...or two... you recommend?

DAN: Uh, sure. (They stand close to one another, lightly touching shoulder to shoulder. Dan can smell her hair.) Hey, Richard...

RICHARD: Yeah. Why don't I-

DAN: Stay here. I'm going to go grab us some breakfast burritos. You hungry?

AMELIA: I'd love a breakfast tamale.

DAN: Done. At Couch World, all your dreams come true. Show Amelia the Scott Baio Collection.

(He exits.)

RICHARD: This denim loveseat is called The Chachi...

(Lights fade as Richard shows Amelia the book.)

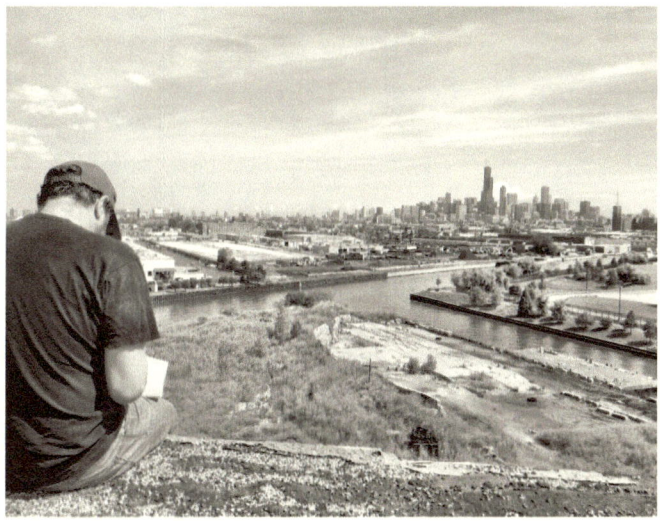

Joe Janes is an Emmy award winning writer and teaches comedy writing and improvisation at The Second City and Columbia College. He has written for Jellyvision's *You Don't Know Jack* and SNL's *Weekend Update*. He has written three books: *365 Sketches, 50 Plays* and *Seven Deadly Plays*. His full-length plays include *Metaluna and the Science of the Mind Revue, A Hard Day's Journey Into Night* and *Always Never*. He writes regularly for WNEP Theatre and Robot vs Dinosaur. You find out what's going on in his world at joejanes.blogspot.com and follow him on Twitter @joejanes1065.

Joe's other books, *365 Sketches* and *50 Plays*, are available at Quimby's Bookstore in Chicago, The Second City Training Center - Chicago and on-line at lulu.com